# THE GUIDED WORD
POWERHOUSE COLLECTION

The Powerhouse Collection:

*A Collection of Poems & Reflections on Empowerment & Healing*

A Division of *The Guided Word*

Copyright 2022 by Beatrica Vasic

All right reserved, including the right to reproduce this book or portions thereof in any form whatsoever.

For information, address *hello@theguidedword.com*

First *The Powerhouse Collection* trade eBook published in July 2022. These books are registered trademarks of Beatrica Vasic

For information about special discounts or bulk purchases, please contact Sales at *hello@theguidedword.com*

Published in Canada
ISBN: 978-1-7782379-2-8

*For anyone who is bold enough to chase a dream they're crazy in love with...*

*With all their heart.*

*Poetry is an experience*
I want to be on your shelves and in your house
In your mind and in your hands

*Remember who the fuck you are.* Wake up. Take back your power. Do it for you. Do it for humanity. Because we need more healing in leadership. We need more compassion in leadership. We need more heart in leadership. We need you to step into the role that was always meant for you and do it exactly how only you can do it. You're not competing with anyone. You're stepping into what has always been yours. I don't know what you have to overcome. I don't know what you have to let go of. I don't know what you have to get yourself out of. I don't know what you have to heal. *I do know that your seat at the table is waiting for you.* And that you'll get there your way and on your timing. I don't know what you're dealing with now. But you were always meant to prosper. *This was never your undoing.*

*I know maybe you're not where you want to be.* Maybe this point in your life is called "the process". It involves believing, doing, acting for the thing you are believing for but not quite seeing the fruits of your labour materialize. It's the part of the movie with the fast-paced montage that skips over all the time it takes to really build something of value. Skip to the exciting part. The good part. The process requires discipline, faith, consistency, and resilience. It's not glamorous. There is an aching, perhaps. You have the vision, but you have no idea how to get there. And every day it seems like you're fighting distraction, disbelief, unworthiness, and fear. It's the place where the everyday mundane feels like it's chipping away at your passion and your soul. It's the place where a lot of people give up. I hope you don't. I hope you fight to keep your passion and your excitement for life. For the life you're going to have. I hope you keep building. Sneaking off and stealing moments in between the things on your to-do list. Because there's so much happening behind the scenes that you don't know about. I hope you keep building and believing and dreaming. I hope you don't hand off your dream to the mundane and resolve to a life of hopelessness and limitation. In those moments of giving up, I hope you know that you were always meant to get through this. You were always meant to prevail.

This is for the *strong ones* who had to pay the price for their strength in ways only they know about. *The ones who are praised for their strength,* but no one ever talks about the *mental anguish* you may have had to go through to acquire that strength. I see you. I feel you.

*I'm sorry for what you went through.*

You're allowed to fall apart. You're still strong if you do. You don't have to carry everyone and take care of everyone all the time to prove your strength.

*You don't have to keep trying to fix broken things.*

*Her*

When I write, the voice comes from another place. A place of knowing.

The voice that has witnessed all the past hurts and traumas I've suppressed. All the heartbreak I've forgotten.

But she's also seen the future.
She knows about our rising. She knows about our thriving.

And every time I put pen to paper, she tells me stories:

*The ones I have forgotten because they hurt too much.*
*The ones I have forgotten because they aren't from this life.*
*And the ones I have yet to revel in. To rejoice in.*

When I write, I am closer to her.
She puts me on the path of becoming.
Your gifts will lead you there too.

## Negotiating with yourself

*The real you:* can I come out?
*The socially acceptable you:* No, not right now. You're at a business meeting. Later.

*The real you:* how about now?
*The socially acceptable you:* No, not now. You're at a social gathering with all your esteemed peers and colleagues. Later.

*The real you:* now?
*The socially acceptable you:* No, family dinner. It's inconvenient. Let's keep the peace.

*The real you:* Now??? You're alone now.
*The socially acceptable you:* I don't know how to be you anymore. I don't remember how.

*The real you:* That's okay. I'll wait until you get tired of pretending to be all these other people.

*You'll find me when you've had enough of being everyone else.*

*Why you never started*

It's easier to spend our lives failing at the things we're told that *we should want*. If we started failing at the things we actually want, it would be too personal.
You would be exposed.
It would hurt too much.

If we never try, the dream is still a possibility.
But that way, it *always stays a dream*.

*Before you give up*

The spaces that are meant for you will not be the same without you. I get that's hard to see right now. But don't let the obstacles cloud your judgement. Yes, they may seem big. Yes, you may be tired. Rest is part of the game plan. But before you exercise your free will and give up, don't forget to consider the anointed impact you'll have when you step into the industries God has called you to. Your impact is required. But only you decide if you want to move forward. If you want *more*. If you will *let* abundance settle over your life like rain.

I trust myself. After all the self-doubt and worry, I need to trust myself. I trust that I have discernment when it comes to my relationships and opportunities. I trust that when I fall short, I will learn and do better. I will lead in the places I am called to lead. When the right opportunities come up and they have me feeling unqualified and insecure, *those are for me*. I can figure it out. I have the capacity to *stretch and expand* for the big things I am called to. When it comes to the impossible, I am the woman for the job. No job or industry dictates my success. I conquer the external by what I carry within me.

To the wounded healer,
You walk around carrying the losses and heartbreak of those you cared for.
What a vision you are.
A sight for sore hearts.

Now, let their burdens go.
Drop everything that is not yours.
Drop everything that hurts.
And heal yourself.
*You don't owe anyone your heart.*

I know you have every reason in the world to harden. To build a thick concrete wall between your heart and the rest of the world so you can keep the disappointments, the hurt, and the pain at a distance. To keep it outside of you. To disassociate from your own emotions. I know it's tempting. It may even feel easy. *I know you have every reason to do it.* What you have been through, what you have been *carrying,* is *heavy.* I understand that. But I hope you don't harden. *Lighter days are up ahead.* A new creation will be born in the light.

Sometimes the greatest act of self-care is walking away from a seemingly "okay" situation that offends your soul every day and betting on yourself. Drowning out every single piece of well-meaning advice that tells you to stay. And listening to the voice that says "This is not for me." This was never for me. But I am going to trust that if I start running in the right direction, what I am seeking will start running towards me too. *Momentum.*

We like to think that it's easier to pretend you don't want the dream. Because if I allowed myself to want it, I would worry about how it could never happen. I would worry about whether I'm good enough and what other people will think of me. And the worry would just eat me up and swallow me whole *on the inside.* Yeah, you may think that if you kill the dream yourself, you have more control over the feeling than if you go after it and the world stomps it out of you, but you're wrong. Because the only things that will never come true with absolute certainty are the things you ruin for yourself before you even try. And trying and failing will never hurt as much as the haunting feeling that you could've given it your all, but you *volunteered to take yourself out of the running for the things that were meant for you.*

Sometimes the road to receiving love looks a lot like unearthing wounds.

*The things you had cast aside and thought you had moved on from.*

Here's to the ones who have had a tumultuous love affair with their dreams since they were children:

You were gifted a map. You were gifted codes to create that which has yet to be created for a reason. *It's supposed to come through you.*

Words for a book,

drawings for a building,

sketches for a design,

brush strokes for a painting,

plans for a business.

And even though the lines of the map seem blurry, the instructions get clearer as you commit to building.

They are linked to the remembrance of who you are. Even as you read these words, you know it. There is something in your body triggering *remembrance* of *your divine destiny.*

*Your soul knows*

Isn't it beautiful
that there is something inside us all
that *speaks softly* to us and
lets us know we are in the presence
of something or someone, *we have forgotten that we love?*

A soul we are meant to love
A passion that we are meant to follow
A truth buried deep inside us
A place to call home

Isn't it neat how our minds can be wiped clean
But we have souls that never forget
To trigger remembrance in our bodies.

## *Anointing*

Come, there is always space for you.
Even if they tell you the market is saturated
or there are plenty of others like you.
*That's not true*
There is only one you.
There is only one you who will do it like you were meant to do.

Writers won't stop writing just because there are other writers out there, *other books*.
Painters won't stop painting just because there are other painters out there, *other paintings*.
Singers won't stop singing just because there are other singers out there, *other songs*.

*Come,* your gifts make space for you.
They were gifted on purpose. They were gifted *with responsibility*.
Come, yes, there is a table for you.

The divine has already marked your spot.
It's just up to you to *take up space*.

Step into your anointing. Bless all who lay eyes on your creation.

The easiest way to turn a blessing into a burden is to dress it up in pressure and obligation. When the opportunity comes up, you don't have to wonder if you're good enough or spin your wheels trying to prove it. *You were made for this*. The path was carved out for you. This is a partnership. You're allowed to do the divine work from a state of peace and ease. You can get the blessing without thinking you need to spend every waking moment proving you're worthy of this opportunity. You can work towards the divine destiny without living in a constant state of distress. Only you can give yourself this permission.

Sometimes it can be scary to live a heart-centred life if your life has been riddled with heartbreak and hurt. Watching people stomp on your heart or betray your trust provides good incentive not to lay it bare in front of others. It provides good incentive to build that concrete wall between your heart and the outside world. But I want you to know that hiding your magnificent heart will hurt just as much as heartbreak. It's a slow numbing over time that robs you of all of life's joys and who you're meant to be. *Guard your heart.* Use *discernment.* But don't remove it from the equation.

As you try to figure out who you are in this life, people will bombard you with well-meaning questions about your destination. Some of these questions may include, but are not limited to: Who will you be? What will you do? When will you grow up? Who are you? Who will you be with? When will you buy the house? Will you get the promotion? What education will you pursue? How many children will you have? When? With whom?

And this will throw you off. Because life is about the journey of figuring things out. Choosing what you will pursue with your whole heart and what you will opt-out of. And then changing your mind. *Growing as you go.*

And you will inevitably feel pressured into *having certainty* around the answers you provide to these questions. *Don't let their questions about your destination dictate your direction.* Don't let their pressure become your map. The map for your journey has always been within you. The time it takes to get to where you want to be is more important than rushing in the wrong direction. *You may believe you will be ok living your life going in the wrong direction as long as it looks good on the outside and silences the questions,* but you won't. Don't drop off your path to becoming to give people, who don't know who they are themselves, some answers to their curiosities.

I used to roll my eyes when people said everything happens for a reason. It's one of those things that we say to comfort people when something devastating happens and we don't know how to help. Until I had lived through enough losses and celebrations to notice a pattern. To see that the cliché was true. Every single heart-shattering disappointment was setting the stage for a blessing or rerouting me to the path that was meant for me. Because sometimes, nothing can motivate you to move differently in your life like an epic heartbreak. Other times, the disappointments or roadblocks were cultivating something within me. A necessary ingredient for my recipe for success. *It was actually in all the hardship that I tried to pray away that I had built all my favourite things about myself.* If you're going through a season of hardship, maybe you're building too.

For the woman that has been called "too much",

Baby, I hope you are a raw display of human emotion. A fountain of expression.
I hope you pour out empathy, compassion, and sadness.
I hope you have *passion* and *determination*.
*No more numbing to make society comfortable.*
And it will, in fact, be too much for some people.
That is because those people have not yet dealt with their own emotions.
Have grace for them.

In a world that enjoys shaming us for where we aren't yet,
*I hope you celebrate how far you've come.*
How much your heart has endured.
How many times you could have given in,
*but you didn't.*

*Liberate yourself in small ways first.* Cancel plans if you need to take care of yourself. Ugly cry. Snot and all, *if you need to*. Be softer with your body and accept that healing takes patience. Don't force your body to contort itself in ways that don't feel good. Some days require Yin Yoga, not an aggressive workout. Take the day off. And if you can't take a day, take an hour. Breathe. *Ask for help,* I know you've always done it all on your own but you don't need to. Whisper kind words to yourself if the world has been unkind to you today.

*Small liberations turn into a life of freedom.* Speak your needs and boundaries. Choose to believe in your own capabilities even if people around you do not, *that's kindness to your future self.* Walk away. Leave, if needed. Slip away from the party early without saying goodbye. Or, don't go at all. Hydrate. Stop forcing yourself to go places you know you have no business going anymore. *Stop letting people use their emotions as a weapon to silence you.* Don't stunt your growth to keep relationships you know you've outgrown. Make time for your faith.

*And other things you've been aching to do, but you think you need permission.*

*Softness requires strength.*

Our society equates strength with hardening.
With experiencing hardships and creating a hard exterior around your *soft spots*.
*Toughen up.* Develop *thicker skin.*

But it takes real strength to experience the brokenness and sorrow in the world,
*to hold it and feel it,*
and still run into the world raw and wide-eyed.
*Ready to experience it all fully:*
the hard places,
but also the ones filled with joy and love,
*(the ones that make life worth living)*
with open vulnerability.
*To expand with them.*

Softness,
sweetness, and
tenderness,
in the face of all that this world is, demands the greatest strength of all.

*Your softness is required in rigid environments.*

I cannot be the woman required for this next part of my journey and simultaneously sit around requiring everyone to validate my decisions.

I can't afford to compare myself to anyone else, it costs too much.

I need to stay in my God-given lane.

I need my eyes to be fixed on the few things that matter and focus, otherwise, it all becomes blurry.

I can't afford indecision. I can't afford to ignore my intuition.

I can't afford to neglect myself and my rest.

*It costs too much.*

*My dearest empath,*

Before you get down on yourself about how sensitive you are, I want you to think about what a gift it is to be able to tap into anyone's emotions.

To understand them in ways others cannot,

to connect with them in ways they aren't even able to express.

*To heal the beings of this earth.* You are a gift to this world.

You think that because *it can cripple you,* it must be a weakness.

I'm telling you it was a power gifted to you because

*you have the capacity to expand enough to hold it.*

I'm okay with *l o n g i n g* for the desires of my heart.

Because I know they *l o n g* for me too.

Together, we'll make our way toward each other.

*A sweet and sultry love affair.*

We'll dance until we meet.

Until we're one again.

Have you been fighting the beautiful person you're growing into by being the version of you that someone you care for needs you to be? Specifically, smaller? Do they need you to be less? Or worse, do you find yourself fighting the person you want to be in order to be more digestible for your acquaintances? *Their temporary approval is not as valuable to you as your ego may trick you into thinking it is.*

*Bloom anyway.*

*The Conundrum of the Artist*

How do I give you enough of me to make good art, *to shake you and make you feel something*, while also keeping a piece of me to myself?

A word about *risk* - Risk is in the eye of the beholder. I've had people tell me I'm taking a risk by walking away from things that didn't serve me. "Stay on the safe path". With what is familiar. Then I got to the other side and saw all the things I gained by walking away from safety. I saw the *risk* of what I could have potentially missed out on if I had stayed with the safe thing that didn't serve me. *A whole life,* I would have missed out on. *Now I see the risk associated with staying in the same place.* The things I *risk* missing out on if I hold onto clutter. *The risk of never having what my heart desires by staying with what I know for certain makes me miserable.* That risk should scare you far more than the unknown.

They come like thieves in the night
to steal the *execution* of your dreams.
*The promise.*
The trio: comparison, perfectionism and fear.
They disguise themselves as logic and practicality.
*The ego is keeping you safe.*

You'll wake in the morning thinking it was all your idea,
(*giving up is sound judgement because that executing your dream seems inconvenient*)
when in fact, your mind was invaded.

Guard your mind by wrapping yourself in light.

I hope that you can *let go* of the person you had to be when you lived in *survival mode*

And activate the *version of you* that's meant to live your life in *thriving mode.*

*It isn't always going to be like this.*

*Actually,*

you're allowed to bleed over things you thought you had healed and still call it

*progress.*

*Stop limiting yourself by seeking the past everywhere you go.*
Your future looks nothing like your past.
The places you're going look nothing like the places you've been.
Stop looking for old loves in new loves.
Stop sabotaging your potential by looking to old habits.
You have no business seeking your new self in your old self.

*Who you've been is nothing compared to the fullest expression of who you are.*

You can't control every thought you have.
But you can control what thoughts you *feed* and let *live inside you*. You can choose the thoughts you adopt as your truth and identity.

Let the loving thoughts build a home inside your mind and treat the destructive thoughts as *unwelcome visitors*.
Just passing through.

*Speak life to who you are.*

*Allow* love.

*Allow* guidance.

*Allow* grace.

*Allow* success.

*Allow* abundance.

*Allow* faith.

*Allow* friendship.

*Allow yourself* to dream again.

*Allow* what you desire to come into your life,

and it'll flow like a river.

*Actually,* I found my power in everything I thought would ruin me. Everything I thought was *designed to break me.*

Thank you.

*Following your heart*

Even if it doesn't work out exactly how I planned,

every step of the way,

I am becoming more m y s e l f

than I ever was before.

*What a worthy pursuit.*

*Affirmations for those who are struggling*

I am always being led.
Even when it looks like I am lost,
I am following the path set out by my soul.

I am still being guided,
even if it feels like e v e r y t h i n g is falling apart.
Even when everything is crumbling around me,
when it doesn't make sense,

I am still being led.

Lessons on *fixing people*:

Once upon a time, two broken people fell in love.

In the end, they only left each other more broken.

Here is your reminder that you don't heal yourself by covering your wounds *with shards of broken glass*.

Show me where they wounded you,

where you think the scars have

*disfigured you.*

That's where the light will come through.

That's where grace will enter.

That's where healing will envelop the pain and hold you.

That's where new life will bloom again.

I wish you healing for all the things you think you cannot recover from,
for all the things you cannot change,
for the scars you're ashamed of,
for the times you fell short,
for the memories that leave a tightness in your chest and you don't know why.
*Healing. Healing. Healing*
You're not doing it alone.
Just call on God, the Universe,
*whatever light you believe in.*
Call on it. Let the light in. Let the light in.
You are so loved.

Love Yourself.
Because if anyone else
supported you,
carried you,
cried for you,
fought for you,
bled for you,
like you do for yourself,
you would love them.
So why not,
love
you?

*Your Gifts*

Honour the universe by using them.
They were given to you at birth.
All wrapped up with your name on them.
Unique to you, my love.
They will keep whispering your name.
Patiently waiting
until you give in,
until you remember,
*what was always a part of you.*

*Pay attention to your gifts,*
unwrap your gifts,
*and let them be your guide.*
You are divine.

*Growing Pains*

The discomfort of stretching further than you currently are, but only seeing and experiencing what you've always experienced. *When the external world does not yet match the transformation in your mind and your heart.* When your mind expands, but your circumstances look the same.
When the people around you *haven't fully embraced the upgrade*.
When you wonder if *you have awakened* or
if you just imagined it all.

*Keep Blooming Anyway.*

*Your gifts existed within you before the world discovered them.*

They continue to reside in you even if the validation and applause disappear.

You're the only one who can give your power away to something external. But I know you know better than that.

*I've seen you come out of dark and desolate places, basking in light.*

Underdogs don't walk away from the fight just because they're unequipped in resources, they *rise to the occasion* and win by leaning into what they've got.

Your determination creates paths where none existed before.

Don't tell me you're going to surrender that to the external.

*No, you're the type that always comes back swinging.*

*You lead by example.*

You lead by showing up with integrity. You lead by kindness. By empathy. *You lead by being strong enough to be vulnerable.* To understand duality and hold it in your vessel. You lead by being powerful enough to speak truth from your heart that shifts the consciousness of those around you.

Your authenticity doesn't need to be sold or marketable.

*This type of authority comes from embodying you, not the latest trend.*

*Never be ashamed of where you started.* You can point to it and say look at what I created. I created from a place filled with nothingness and I made *abundance*. I *created* what never existed through pure *grit* and *divine guidance*. I created an empire from scratch.

*And now my nothingness will feed generations.*

Just because it was necessary doesn't mean it didn't hurt.
Just because it will lead you to better things doesn't mean that the loss doesn't gut you.
There were some things you had to let go of to get here that you thought you would have forever.
*That you thought you could rely on.*
Let yourself grieve that.
Let yourself grieve that life.
Even if you chose to let them go.
Don't let anyone negate your feelings with *"it's for the best."*
Choice doesn't negate your feelings.
You're allowed to feel.
*We move on in stages and waves.*

I believe deeply in the magic of the universe. That doesn't mean that I am immune to the disappointments of life. I believe deeply in God and His divine timing and protection. That doesn't mean I am immune to pain, suffering, and anxiety. What it means is that whenever I stray too much in my broken humanness, there is an unconditional love that consoles me. Wipes my tears and grounds me into the loving earth. Pulls me back into the present moment

and *brings me back to life*.

*Shadow Work*

I am trying to heal.
I am looking at the darkness in me
and trusting that the darkness won't swallow me whole.
I am looking at the darkness and *all the brokenness* to make space for the light,
and I am trusting that I can *let more light shine through.*
That I can take *what's broken* and alchemize it
*into divine energy.*

It was the moment that I started to pray about *not getting* opportunities that I knew weren't good for me, but I wasn't strong enough to refuse them in that season of my life, that I started to truly understand that every rejection is actually a blessing in disguise.

Every rejection is a redirection.

*Divine protection.*

*How to release the pressure of "first"*

We tend to overemphasize firsts and load them with a ton of pressure. The first book, the first song, first job, first opportunity, first kid, first house, first course, first release, first love. We put so much pressure on ourselves to have the perfect first draft that we cannot possibly live up to the standard we've set in our minds. So often we decide that there's no other course of action than to scrap it all before we experience immense ridicule. The concept of getting it right on the first try can drive you mad and stifle your creativity. Unless you perform well under crushing pressure. Instead, think about the first as the first of many. One of many successful books you'll write. The first in a series of subsequent successes. That get better and juicer over time. If we stop desperately clutching to the idea that we only have one shot at everything in life, we can release the pressure and let creativity and innovation come through.
So we can have longevity. Consistency.
*Sustainable growth and success.*

I don't need you to choose me.
I have already chosen myself.
I've already *c r o w n e d*
myself *worthy*.

I believe we choose if we walk in our destiny. Our path. Our purpose. I believe we absolutely have free will. I believe that certain things are pre-ordained, but we make our own choices to step into them. I also believe that everything we are seeking - *our destiny* - is desperately trying to get our attention when we are on the wrong path. Through our hearts, souls, conversations, songs, signs, and events. The things you keep calling "a coincidence." It chose you. *It wants you to choose it back.* What's meant for us is always creating paths for us to come back to it. Calling us back to *what we always knew in our hearts.*

I think that the things that are meant for you, *the ones that make you feel alive,* are a part of you.
*Balloons attached by string to you,*
pulling your head and heart above you,
*straight to the clouds.*
Way past what the eye can see on the ground.
And closer to the "impossible."
They bring us closer to the *universe.*
Your gifts will take you where you need to go.

*Your gifts will take you where you need to go*

If you told me that I would be writing these words 4 years ago, I would have thought that you were playing a seriously fucked up joke. Some dreams are so dear to us that we need to shield them from the harsh light of "reality." They seem so unimaginably unattainable to us, based on our conditioning, that we have to shove them in glass jars deep in our minds. For protection, they are never to be touched or thought of. But, I have found that even when tucked away in the crevices of our unconscious, *tucked away in a security blanket of limiting beliefs,* the things that are meant for us still have a way of unconsciously leading us to paths to reclaim them. Over and over again, no matter how many times we walked away.

I believe that every moment here on earth
is a living and breathing prayer.
So be *intentional* about
what you're *praying* for.

*Writer's High*

When you find the right words. When a truth hidden deep in my subconscious is unlocked and released. When I know this was planted in me for a purpose. When I know this one's for me just as much as it is for you, *darling reader*. We're sharing an experience, you and I. When something heals inside me through this emotional purge. When the artist bleeds their heart out on paper and the poison turns into someone else's peace. When hurt is alchemized into love. Because the words wield power.
*Because the right words change everything.*

I believe you found me for a reason.
Your heart settled here for a reason.

I believe that some words are spells.

Activating divine destiny and magic.

You never know when you'll receive them or when you'll be tasked with gifting them to another.

At any given moment there are different versions of us walking around - the ones that are hurt and weighed down by the disappointment and torment this life can bring,
the ones who have healed and found that love is the ointment for all their aches and pains,
the ones reaching out for the desires of their heart, despite all the fear invading their minds,
*the ones thriving.*
At any given moment, we can decide to snatch up any of these versions of ourselves and embody them. *Let them be your guide to where you want to go.*

Daily, a war is waged in me:

The lawyer and the writer.
The realist and the dreamer.
The cynic and the believer.
Right brain and left brain.
The masculine energy and the feminine energy.
The mind and the heart.
The critic and the creator.

*I need them to call a ceasefire if I am ever to be whole.*
*I need them to co-exist peacefully if I am ever to be whole.*

At some point in time, I am not sure even when it happened, but I found myself developing an aversion to seeing certain people who were once important to me in my life.

Because I didn't want them pulling out the old versions of me that I didn't resonate with or care for anymore.

Ones that triggered negative thought patterns and habits I had ditched, just with the power of their presence. Conjuring up old ghosts I *thought* I had parted with.

My resistance to them was my commitment to letting go of the version of myself unconsciously flaring up in their presence.

I had to let some things go
simply because I wanted to spend
more time
operating out of my heart,
*rather than my mind.*

I am *grateful*

for everything I have.

But I am still coming for those

*locked doors* with

my name on them.

I think a lot of our industries are set up in a disempowered way that requires you to perform and depend on being chosen to succeed. The *"pick me"* industries. The ones that are designed to keep some people out and let some people in. *The gatekeepers of power.* Power bouncers. You need to be chosen to come inside. Pay your dues. Perform for approval or *be denied entry.* And we repeat this cycle. Over and over again. *It doesn't stop when you gain access and entry to this elite realm.* Performance is conditional to your stay. You continue. Jumping through hoops to get someone to pick us. To validate us. Choose us. Until we forget who we are. Here's some encouragement - you take your power back when you decide you don't need anyone to pick you to be worthy. You have chosen yourself. You have crowned yourself worthy. You are here to help build and design a new power structure. Trust yourself.

The voice of an influential woman in her power cannot be borrowed. It can't be taken from someone else and regurgitated. *No copy and pasting.* It's also recognized by others, like the anointing in her life. It's distinct. *Activating destiny in the lives of those she was meant to serve.* She weaves healing spells with her words. Her influence comes from the deep knowing within her, not what she has been fed by the world. It's impactful because it comes from her. It was unlocked within her body, in her relationship with the divine. A woman who trusts herself is a force to be reckoned with. *She speaks honey truths.* You have the key, you just need to open up. But my *darling,* the voice of influence cannot come from the outside. You cannot allow it to get lost in all the information and voices you consume. Rise up. *You were born for this.* You cannot speak about what they want you to speak about or package it in the neat and comprehensible way they demand. Your authentic voice demands truth - everything, from the words down to the tone, is all uniquely yours. So if you're going to answer the call to lead I suggest you stop borrowing words.

*I used to be fiercely loyal.* To a fault. When I would fully let someone into my heart, there was nothing I wouldn't do for them. There was no boundary between you and me. If you needed a friend at 3 am to call and vent your heart out about a bad date, I would be there. If you needed someone to drop everything and be there for you, I would be there. If you needed me to pick you over anything or anyone else in my life, I would do it. There was also no behaviour I wouldn't excuse or defend. Because we're like family, right? The same goes for romantic partners. *Ride or die, right?* I eventually learned, through a lot of heartbreak, that this type of loyalty was rarely reciprocated. And if I was being truthful, *I shouldn't have expected it either.* It was a convenient one-way street. The love I was pouring into others was not being returned and that would leave me *empty and bitter.* I realized that maybe it was because that love and loyalty were always meant for me. I *was meant* to pour that into my own empty crevices. The places I was lacking, those were the places that I was supposed to pour into. *I should have been that fiercely loyal to myself.* And it made for much better and healthier relationships. These days, when the phone rings at 3 am, I let it ring. And I'm okay with that.

*I am pursuing my heart's desires.* Not so I can prove to anyone how wrong they are about me or what I am capable of. *This has nothing to do with anyone else.* I don't have anything to prove. I'm doing it so I can reassure myself that I've got her back and I'm willing to do what it takes to support her heart in ways no one else did. Supporting her heart, supporting her God-given vision. I want her to know *she is loved.*

My love language is supporting myself and giving myself permission to go after what I've felt called to for a long time, instead of standing in my own way. Standing in the way of my own happiness, of my ability to experiment and play, standing in the way of what feels fulfilling to me. I'm not here to tell her she's not good enough. *She has the world for that.* I am playing for her team and it's time that my *actions and thoughts* show it.

*It's time to let go of any remnants of self-sabotage.*

*When revelation comes for your heart*

When revelation comes for your heart and mind,
it will get harder to hold onto things that do not align.

It may require that you end some conversations, walk out of some rooms, and end some relationships.
Because it physically hurts to hold on.
It drains you, and the harder you try to make yourself fit those things again *out of nostalgia,* the more painful it will be.

Nothing forced, it just happens organically. Because the person you were when you chose that life is different from who you are now.

Years of thoughts and prayers require action now. There's momentum. The timing is right.

*But that doesn't mean you can't grieve the good things you've outgrown from your past life.*
You're allowed to grieve the things and people you've outgrown.
Mourn them. Bless them. Thank them.
*Oh, how they served you for the season you were in.*

*A new outcome comes from a new choice*

A lot of people told me that they loved me and left me
before I could become the woman
who stopped *choosing* people
who said they loved me then
*left me.*

The goal was never for you to pay attention to me.

The goal was to change how you think.

I want to leave you better than I found you.

I want you tapping into *revolutionary thought patterns*.

I want these words to *pierce through the noise*, cut right through the confusion, and remind you how infinitely powerful you are.

*How the energy inside you is matched only by the ocean's t i d e.*

Pursuing can also mean:
listening,
breathing,
healing,
and *dancing with the universe.*
Taking a step forward in faith and
*knowing* when to step back
so that the cosmic forces conspiring in your favour can step in.

*This dance requires you to take the steps, but also know when to surrender to your partner's lead.*

*Why I won't let you pick me:*

I spent my whole life trying to get people to pick me.

Jobs, relationships, friendships, opportunities.

I lived in a system of disempowerment and performance.

*Perform my best so that you can crown me worthy.*

Tell me I am smart and capable because I can jump through hoops and score on metrics.

*Be agreeable in relationships so you won't get mad enough to leave me one day.*

So you won't get fed up with my honesty and decide that I'm not worth the trouble.

So I will be the woman who pretends she doesn't need anything from you to buy us more time.

If I don't need anything there would be no reason for you to leave.

Then I found my worth in all the heartbreak and realized that I had to start choosing.

I had to stop asking other people to see my value and *pick myself.*

I won't let you pick me because, in order to operate from my highest version of myself, I need to choose.

I need to start making choices. Take accountability for where my life is going.

*So no, I'm sorry, but I can't let you pick me.*

*Your journey into the dark was never meant to break you.* It was meant to teach others the way back to the light. You were always meant to come out of this. You were always meant to overcome. To prosper. It was written before the beginning of time. This was never your undoing. Carry this in your heart through the trials.

Wait for the opportunity,

wait for the person,

that has the universe written all over it.

You know the one

that's tailored exactly for you.

*Unmistakably yours.*

Perfect in ways you never allowed yourself to dream of.

Like the universe and all the stars conspired in your favour.

Because the universe dreamed it up for you.

*Wait for the manifestation that is unmistakably yours.*

Sometimes, you need to let it all fall apart. Let it come crashing down. Let it break. Burn it to the ground. Release it. What do you feel obligated to stubbornly hold onto, even though it drains the life out of you? Are you being called to let it go? Rid yourself of the toxicity you've held onto for so long that you don't recognize a life without it. Surrender it. Pray about it.
*And trust that you're making room.*

The universe is my best friend. It has gotten me out of so many messes of my own creation. It has surprised me and delighted me how beautifully things can work out when I'm not trying to control everything. It has always been there for me, even if I haven't prayed or checked-in in a while. Even when I lose faith or I'm impatient, God and the universe are always smiling down at me. Showering me with unconditional love. Doesn't matter if I felt I was insecure and unworthy that day. If I'm mad because I don't understand how this can all be unfolding in my favour. No matter what. The universe has always had my back. Like it has everyone's back. Like it loves everyone. I know I can trust that if I have been called to something, I will be delivered through it.

*You've changed,* they said.

Well yes, it's true. I couldn't be the person that pretended to be void of needs and opinions so that I could make everyone else in the room more comfortable. *To buy more time in my relationships.* I couldn't shrink myself any further to fit in the container.

*It turns out, I am actually expansive.* I couldn't keep choking on words. I couldn't keep people-pleasing.

*I found out I couldn't keep betraying myself and step into who I am meant to be.*

The relationships that last will bloom even if you express needs and opinions that are contradictory to theirs.

*Reminders from your heart*

You hold so much within me.
Anguish, love, suffering, joy.
Your lifeblood pumps through me,
*flowing life into your magnificent existence.*
K e e p i n g  y o u  a l i v e.
I've taken beatings and bruisings in your pursuit of love.
Everything you've ever felt is kept in memories stored within me.
I crack when you cry.
I am the key to your healing.
I am your connection to all that is divine in this life.
Protect me. Guard me. Don't give me away to just anyone.

*But, keep me open.*

*You are the universe's favourite story.*

If it seems like your life has been marked with struggle and seasons of drought, pay close attention.
Your triumph happens when the odds are stacked against you, *everyone has written you off,* and when it looks like you've lost.
Your victory rises from ashes and ruins in destitute places.

*Yours is the story of the underdog.*

Dear cycle breaker,

How exhausting it is to keep tackling that which brought generations before you to their knees, seeking freedom from the mental shackles that kept them bound in a new world that looks nothing like the one your ancestors knew.
Let the burdens go. Let the patterns go. Let the trauma go. Let the agony go.
Let them go.
Your job is to be strong enough to carry the wounds forth into this final generation
and soft enough to drop them.
*Chosen.*
To hand them over to the divine and say "we don't need this anymore."
We don't need the pain and suffering anymore.
It ends here.

Sweet child, how exhausted you must be.
Lay your head down and rest your eyes.
Let God's peace in.

Sometimes in the frantic pace of life and consumption, your heart craves a season of solitude.
You don't really want to go out,
you don't want to chase highs and distractions anymore.
The stimulation of everyday life can become overwhelming and bombard your nervous system.
This season, you crave to know yourself internally and cultivate peace.
If this season has come for you, please don't judge yourself and be concerned.
Sometimes, some quiet alone time can be medicine for the heart and soul.
Don't force yourself to go out or pretend to be extroverted during this season when you're just not feeling the bright lights, loud music or small talk.
You're allowed to give yourself some grace. Always.

It'll happen when you release the pressure. The pressure of timelines. *It's not happening fast enough.* The pressure of perfection. The pressure for it to look a certain way. The pressure to please anyone. The pressure to perform. The pressure that requires emotional validation.

*As soon as you release the pressure, what's meant for you will start making its way to you.*

Trust is medicine.

Trust is medicine. It's the ointment for a stressed-out and burnt-out mind. Exhausted and overworked from the hamster wheel of consumption, expectations, and worries. *You worry because you don't trust.* You worry because it's always been hard. *You control because you don't trust.* When you realize that everything will always happen exactly as it should, no matter what path you take, your nervous system starts to calm down. It gets to happen without all the resistance and micromanaging. *Trust is divine medicine.*

I am generating more light from my dark places.

From my *wounded places.*

Generating light.

That's what we do as healers, leaders, lovers, lightworkers, divine beings,

*miracles for the world,*

our light is self-sourced.

Even after all the pain, the devastation,

the light still shines within us

and illuminates the path.

Even when it feels dimmer,

we are always healing.

Ointment for ourselves and others.

Watch how all this light still streams through the cracks of all my broken places.

That's what God placed us here for,

*for such a time as this.*

Life as an artist/empath/highly sensitive human being:

There's no separation between you and me. I feel connected to everything and everyone in this room. I'm bombarded by sensory experiences and vivid colours. My feelings are in HD. When I'm excited, I'm ecstatic. When I'm sad, I feel the weight of everyone's heartache. Cry an ocean for the brokenness of the world. I love on steroids and there's no filter on my energy. Sometimes, I feel so much I need to lie down. I also have the gift of revelling deeply in every experience this life has to offer. *I couldn't stop it if I tried.* But without proper boundaries and proper self-care, this life can take a toll on this human vessel of mine.

*Handle yourself with care, you special and beautiful human.*

Maybe you're actually doing everything right. Maybe you're doing all the steps and you're doing your part. Maybe you're already on the right path and you don't need to spend every moment second-guessing yourself. Maybe the action is right and this is just the story of your life and every single thing you're going through is getting you closer and closer to the person you're supposed to be (*the person you've secretly always been*) and the life you're supposed to live. You just have to let the universe do the rest and trust in what you've been building. *Day by day.* Maybe you're supposed to enjoy yourself more, love harder and trust more deeply. Maybe this is your sign from the universe, "*you're doing alright, kid.*"

*Peter Pan Syndrome*

Have you ever had a dream that you just run away? Leave all your responsibilities behind and live your life with delicious carelessness? Go wherever your heart desires and see what this beautiful world has to offer? Take in landscapes you've only ever seen on canvasses? Maybe you never come back. Maybe you spend your life creating and soaking up every single moment, instead of running away from them. Your life is such a dream that you've probably never been so laser-focused on the present moment and reality. *Isn't that ironic?* Maybe you love with all your heart and dance with the universe. Maybe it's about joy; not about timelines, careers, and fulfilling social obligations that you don't even remember signing up for. Maybe it's all so whimsical and you get swept up in romanticizing your life. Maybe the difference between your current life and your dream is just a series of choices. Always waiting and available for you.

*I hope one day you're brave enough to make your dream a reality.*

When you finally find peace, *will you recognize her face*?

Or will you be busy chasing down the ghost of emotions already passed?

Sometimes I think we're really busy holding on to grudges and memories of the past, trying to vindicate ourselves in snapshots of time that passed long ago and will never return again.

We forget to let peace in when she comes knocking on our door.

*I think I'm afraid of getting older,* I say. But I think what I'm actually afraid of is losing my sparkle. Losing my passion and appetite for life in a heap of responsibilities and bills. I think I'm afraid of unfilled dreams and plans, lost somewhere in conversations passed, a cloud of smoke, and nostalgia. I think I'm afraid to be boring. I think I'm afraid of no longer having the capacity to enjoy the magic in a sunset or the colours in the sky. I'm afraid of betraying myself and losing who I am in small moments. Like I'm floating away with every burden I take on. I'm afraid that the demands on my life and my time will rob me of the childlike joy and wonder I have carried within me up until now. *Growing up looks like a void that will swallow me up once I start and there will be nothing left of this person that I used to be.* I think I'm afraid of losing my freedom. But, I think we forget that these things leave us by choice, not age.

*So I hope you never stop fighting for your aliveness and childlike wonder.*

Truths about healing:

You can be hurt and still move forward.
You can be wounded and still be loved deeply by someone who sees those wounds.
Your scars are a light for those who are still raw and bleeding
You can't avoid pain, but you can choose what it does to your heart.

Please let the right people love you while you heal.

I cannot lose myself. Not really. Because every time I wander, I trust that I will be *g u i d e d* back to where I am supposed to go. Because I always have been. So it's okay to feel lost as long as I know that I am always right on schedule. You cannot screw it up even if you tried. Because this is your life and it's always unfolding exactly as it was meant to. Your soul always finds a way even if you cannot see that right now. Your h e a r t pulls you closer to what you desire. Everything in between is just experience. And that has immense value too, *even if it doesn't feel good in the moment.* Sometimes *e x p a n s i o n* feels uncomfortable. Rising to new levels can feel uncomfortable. But you can know peace if you understand it's *always working out for you* in ways you're on the cusp of discovering. Play in the energy of anticipating *magic*.

*I don't recognize her anymore.* I used to walk into a room and my whole body would contract, unconsciously anticipating that I would spend all night shrinking so that I could get through conversations. How much smaller I would have to get for someone to like me. *Control their perception of me.* Because being my full and expansive self would intimidate people. Because it's better to be small, but have the temporary approval of a bunch of random acquaintances than to stand alone. *That's just how we're wired, right?* Small me, small talk, small impact, small everything. What drink should I order? Should I learn how to play golf to fit in? Should I laugh at that risqué joke to avoid offending anyone?

As I said, I don't recognize her anymore.

*Now I understand that I influence the energy of the room.*

Fuck being small. I own fucking the room.

*Before you decide you're not enough*:

Are you not enough or is it taking *some time*? Are you not enough or are you projecting the instant gratification culture we live in and arbitrary timelines on *your dreams?* Are you not enough or are you leaking all your energy trying so hard to control something as fierce and uncontrollable as the flow of life? *Lean in.* You are built for your purpose. You have every single thing you need within you. You and your purpose are one and the same. You are provided for. You were always built to overcome every single obstacle that comes up along the way on your journey. You were even built to withstand walking away and returning to yourself. The *Rebuilding* process. You were always meant to have a beautiful and expansive life. But you have to choose it, no one can do that for you. You are the only person who can decide to trust yourself.

*Empowerment is owning all the facets of your emotions, not just the positive ones.* The extent to which your consciousness can fully expand is the extent to which you can let all of life in. The reason toxic positivity is so toxic is that it attempts to sever you from the whole. Puts up a resistance to what is rather than awareness of what is. The key is to be able to straddle duality: accept what is while also not dwelling in the darkness. *Living and breathing in it.*

Your wounds open portals,

*they are the keys to your ascension.*

I am a vessel. I am a clear channel for the messages and words that come through me. I am a vessel. I am a channel for magic and divine wisdom. That's why I can trust what I create. It's always meant to come through me. There is no "not good enough". I can trust what is coming through me. I can trust how the divine works through me. *Perfection was never a part of the equation.*

I assume every single thing I am called to do or say has a purpose. Read that again: it has a purpose. *Not an agenda.* I live from the assumption that everything that comes from my heart is there for a reason. Some of the things I do will attract more eyeballs, while others will be disregarded by the many but profoundly impact the few. So I will risk whatever the fear stories in my head tell me might happen and trust the message that I have been entrusted with. There is no "not good enough." That's actually completely irrelevant. When you have been entrusted with a message, a story or a perspective, the way in which you choose to communicate it is exactly how it's supposed to come out.

*Perfection was never a part of the equation.*

*Reinvention*

Nothing new can come into your life until you make *space* for it.
Sometimes walking in your purpose means taking a bulldozer to your life,
*smashing your old identity until nothing remains.*
Other times, it's small, gradual and fierce steps towards freedom.
Celebrate both.
*They take so much courage.*
I promise you, starting over doesn't mean losing.

I was writing this poem and I felt rushed. I was trying to turn it into something. *Hurry the words out of me, so I can move to the next thing I wanted to accomplish in my day.* And I thought about how much of our lives we spend rushing. Contorting, controlling. Speeding up the process so we can *get to the next thing*. The next task. The next part. I was trying to force the poem, rather than leaning into the flow of my creative energy. When really, poetry should be a *decadent experience*. Something luxurious. A finer thing. Can you imagine anything more divine than setting aside a few hours in your afternoon, getting into something that makes you feel beautiful, sitting around with a glass of wine or a latte, and just *basking in the words you're reading*? Romanticizing life through the text? If that's how I want you to feel when you cozy up to this book, then that's the energy I need to bring to the words. To the writing process. But isn't this also how we should feel about our lives? Soaking up the moments and opening to life? Rather than fighting to get through the day, absentmindedly checking off tasks, surviving, controlling, and rushing? We should be making love to the process. Because we cannot enjoy life if we rush through the days, hours, and moments that make up our lives. Writing this piece reminded me that the finer things require our time and selfishly demand our full attention. Give in to your life, give the moments that make up your life your undivided attention.

*Your worth exists independent of any metric for performance.*

Your worth transcends all of the external places you go to measure your progress in life.

Your worth is established outside of all the places you go to seek validation for your existence.

It cannot be negotiated or earned.

*You're worthy because you are.*

*Settle back into yourself*

Come home, come home.
Settle back into yourself.
Remember, please remember.
You are not the weight you carry.
Drop it whenever you want.
Shed your hurts and everything they told you that you had to be.
That's the key.
*Honey, welcome home.*
The greatest wisdom of this universe exists in your body.
*Settle back into yourself.*

I prefer *bold*. I prefer *luxurious*.

I prefer that I set the standard for what I receive from life, rather than letting what I see in the external world dictate who and what I will become.

I prefer *action* that is *bold*.

I desire it so it's mine because I am an energetic match for it.

I prefer a *mind free from limitations*.

I prefer an empowered spirit.

I prefer an abundant life, *a fulfilling life*. I prefer a supportive love. I prefer a life that is expansive and makes me excited to greet the day.

*Honey,* let your preferences be known, you have choices.

The universe is listening.

*Slow living*

Making time to do things intentionally. Savouring every joyful second. Sipping your coffee in the morning while you get lost in its aroma, like your own ritual or form of meditation. Full-belly laughing with friends until the tears come rushing to your eyes. Take a second look at yourself in the mirror and appreciate how well you cleaned up before a night on the town. Good wine. A bubble bath in the middle of the afternoon, just because. A book with no instructional value, just immersing yourself in a story purely out of pleasure. Singing at the top of your lungs when your favourite song, or *any song,* comes on the radio. Simply prioritize joy in the moments available to you. Understand that all things come into your life at the right time, so you don't need to rush anything. You're always on time. The universe wills it so. Your life is a masterpiece and masterpieces take time.

Your life is a masterpiece and masterpieces take time. We've lost that lately in our culture, haven't we? We have sayings like "Rome wasn't built in a day." But now we expect it to be, with the lightning speed everything moves in our instant gratification culture. Amazon prime delivery, fast food, overnight success, hustle, mass work production, mass farming, multi-tasking, and constant access to information. It's all faster than ever before. *Even though our minds weren't made to keep up with such speed.* So we pressure and put expectations on everything in our lives to be that fast. *Instantaneous.* But it still takes time to build trust and a solid relationship, it still takes nine months for a baby to be born, it still takes years to master a craft, it still takes time to build an empire and a reputation, it still takes time to build a home. *The valuable things still take time.* And sometimes, when we no longer have the patience to wait, we decide to settle for much less than a masterpiece. But this is your beautiful life and it's worth the wait. And so I ask you - for the sake of your nervous system, stop putting so much pressure on the things that were always meant to bloom in your life.

What does it mean to be a *powerhouse?*

First off, radical responsibility. Responsibility for your life and the role you play in it. *The way you treat others.* When you know better, do better. With all that power, you better believe you need to match it with responsible and compassionate living. *Help when you can.* God gave you gifts so you can bless others too (no, that doesn't always mean financially).

Second, *integrity.* When you're a powerhouse, people want to live their life like you. So start showing up as someone other people could be modelling their lives after. Inspire good character. If you think your actions are insignificant, you will behave in a way that reflects this belief. *People are watching.*

Third, it means you understand your own value and prioritize your well-being and time. Because you can't achieve anything if your body gives out or you waste all your time. When I say waste your time - sleeping is not a waste. Your energy is the most important asset you have.

Fourth, being a powerhouse means main character energy. Don't accept anyone treating you like you're an extra who could be replaced at any moment.

Fifth, failure doesn't exist. There is nothing anyone can do or say to make you believe that you cannot have the desires of your heart. You are convicted. You can have doubts and bad days, but that is not the place from which you operate regularly. You know deep in your heart, always, that it's just a matter of when.

Sixth, grace for yourself and others. Radical compassion over and over again, so you can keep yourself light. You can't make your mark on the world weighed down by the past. You need to let that go and forgive whoever you need to forgive. That includes yourself.

*Evolve*

I know what I am worth

Because I know settling
Because I know heartache
Because I know insecurity
Because I know powerlessness
Because I know inauthenticity
Because I know hiding
Because I know shame
Because I know lack

The hard place is where you evolve. I know you don't like it here. It's *uncomfortable.*

But you're the sword forged in fire. Remember that.

*Let them go.* Forgive them. I know the resistance is coming up even as you read these words. Listen, holding onto the past is an anchor you simply cannot afford. You have so much waiting for you on the other side of letting go. I know - sometimes it can be family or people who felt like family at one point who hurt you. Maybe you hurt them too and you need to forgive yourself. Whatever it is, your peace is worth the process. Whatever work you need to do, whatever decisions you need to make, whatever changes need to take place. Do it. *Nothing is more painful than holding onto hurt.*

*Nothing is robbing you more than inflicting the past on your present and future.* You don't need to recreate this anymore. The past is over and done. You are worthy of a new life and peace of mind. *You don't need to be so hard on yourself.* Let go of whatever stories or meaning you attached to the outcome of that situation. It doesn't mean anything about what you're capable of or whether you deserve love. Some people are in a season of your life to show you the places within yourself where you do not love yourself enough. To teach you where you need to love yourself more. To point out the places you still need to heal. That is all. They are not a reflection of what you deserve. I'm going to need you to let them go and forgive them, for no other reason than for you to learn to breathe again.

Be a force for good. Be a force for change. We've had enough darkness and brokenness in this world, *we could use a kind soul like you.* We could use a caring heart like yours. You can contribute in small ways - by being present and loving the people closest to you with all your might. By spreading love, *like confetti,* wherever you go. Whenever you remember to do so, *I know we all have a lot on our plates.* By smiling at strangers and holding the door for them. By getting someone's coffee. Picking up the tab at drinks or dinner. Listening when you see someone hurting. Expressing gratitude to the people making an impact in your life. Donate whatever resources you have at your disposal (time, money, knowledge). Sometimes the world's disappointments and trials look insurmountable and make it seem like there's nothing you can do, but I know there's something you absolutely can do for someone. Keep your eyes peeled and your heart open. When you have the intention to help, the universe usually matches you up with someone you can do something for. Thank you for being here, for such a time as this. The collective appreciates you. God sees all you do that man never thanks you for.

It was always you assigning worth. Assigning energetic standards. You assign worth to yourself, to your time, to the clothes you wear, to the work you do. *How do you value yourself? Your time? Access to you?* You assign value. People fall in line accordingly. *Meaning* some people won't look twice at you because your standard is too high for them. *Too expensive in energetic currency.* And in the end, some people come into your life so you can reassess, reconsider, and reassign value accordingly.

You and I, if we have unfinished business, I'll finish it. *It's done.* I don't have time for energetic loose ends. Playing stories in my mind about how scenarios should've played out. I don't depend on other people to give me closure, I'll close it myself. I used to get wrapped up in stories and narratives around the meaning of certain interactions or relationships, I don't do that anymore. *It just was the way it was.* Ouf, I know your brain doesn't like that one. I don't need to break my mind figuring out why it happened or what it means that they didn't give me what I wanted or needed. We don't need to play the overanalyzing game for answers people don't even have themselves. The book is closed, shut it. That chapter, it's finished. *I am the one who has the power to give myself what I need and desire.* I won't attach or beg other people to do me better, I do myself better. If people ghost, don't stress - that's their lack of integrity.

Behind every strong person is a bunch of nights they cried themselves to sleep until they realized they deserved better. *I'm so sorry for what the world did to you, but I'm glad you decided it wouldn't break you.* I know we can't control how other people hurt us, but we can commit to healing ourselves. Being there for ourselves. Treasuring ourselves. Nursing ourselves back to health every moment of every day. Over and over again. It's not going to be perfect. But there's no one more worth it.

To the woman who is *tired*,

You are still a queen,
even when it feels like your kingdom
is in *ruins*.

You will continue to go through hardship and challenges in your life, even once you start living in your power. The only difference is that you do not surrender to the hard times completely. You can hold the duality. The pain of hurts or loss. You may even struggle, but there is a new knowing. A new piece of information. *A certainty you didn't have before:* You got this. You know you can meet life wherever you're at. You always have and you always will. You know that you have God and the universe on your side, and something *strengthens* within you. A deep trust. So, you can fall apart, that's perfectly okay. You can ask for help, that's perfectly okay. Because one way or another you always come out swinging. You're not making decisions from the lens of the scared and helpless child you once were. You are not at the mercy of the external world because what you have within is rock solid and it doesn't change with the winds or the storms.

*Operating from trust and certainty*

I no longer flinch when my calling looks big.
It's big? *Good.*
It's going to take time and work? *Good.*
I do not rush, I take it one step at a time and let my life unfold as it was meant to. I enjoy my life. I will be here, *consistently* doing my thing in a state of awe and gratitude.
I may need rest, but I always come back and continue showing up. *I am devoted to my craft.*
If I don't know something, I'll learn. If something looks complicated, *simplify it.*
I will keep going. I don't need to look at what other people are doing.
If they want to look or talk about me, that is okay. It comes with the territory. It comes with ambition. It comes with greatness. It comes with impact.
Now, I can choose to shrink away in obscurity the second a challenge arises or I can choose to stand firm in the belief that nothing can touch me because that is God's will for my life.

It will not come to you as long as you are straddling two lives. It can't. You can't follow two paths at the same time. Like two lovers who pull your heartstrings in different directions, eventually, *you will have to choose*. The really great things, the big things you want to do - they are going to require faith and *commitment*. They're going to demand all you have to give. All of you. And you can't negotiate your way out of that. So you choose - either step in or step out. But don't think you're going to get there by half-assing your calling.

*The next part of your journey starts whenever you decide.*

When you decide you're going to show up differently. When you decide you're going to believe differently. When you decide you're going to think differently. *When you decide to have different expectations.* When you decide you're going to love differently. When you decide you're going to forgive differently. When you decide you're going to open yourself up to the realm of possibilities.

It all starts with a decision. *The mountain doesn't move until your mind does.*

*Rebirth*

I have waited lifetimes for you to find me.
I hoped and wept with you on your search.
Welcome home. You complete me.
*You are a waterfall of love.*
Everywhere you go, it's spilling out of you.
You are bathed in starlight and divinity.
You are pure magic.
*I've always loved you.*

- Self

Expanding can be painful.
You may literally be *breaking yourself open*
to build a new woman.

To the cycle breakers,

I know what it's like. I know what it's like to hope for something you've never seen happen in the lives of those closest to you. In the place you grew up.
I know what it's like to be the little kid *on the outside looking in*, accepting that there are things that you could never have because you're not like the other kids.

To those who grew up in scarcity and watched destructive relationships in their families, but are trying to make a life better than the ones they have observed, you think:
How can something true for everyone around me not be true for me? It's only ever been this way, it's only ever been hard,
*so how can it be different for me? Let's explore that question.*

You have the hardest task of all. But it doesn't have to be the way it was for everyone before you. I know how hard it is to hope and believe for something you've never seen play out with your own two eyes. You are so worthy of it, cycle breaker. I carry you in my heart. Know that yours is not an easy path only because it is a different one and the beliefs accumulated by those before you often do not serve you.
And even though you may feel lost sometimes, *you are here to blaze the trail ahead for the ones who come after you.*

Replace "what if it doesn't work?" with *actually, I trust myself. I don't entertain notions of it not working out. As I step up, life will meet me at my next level.*

Replace "the market is saturated" with *my place has always been carved out for me. I am willing to put in the work to master my craft.*

Replace "what if they don't like it" with *"my work always finds the people it's meant to serve. My destiny doesn't hinge on the approval of people who do not have my vision."*

The biggest difference between those who achieve a dream and the ones that walk away while they're building something great are the narratives that they allow to run loose through their heads.

I think the way good energy and blessings work is that you put out your gifts and your kindness. *Even if someone else says something negative about you, puts you down or bashes you.* You keep doing good *for yourself.* Because you're a person of integrity.

Then you put out your gifts.
You're drawn to something in this life. You keep coming back to it and it crosses over with something that comes naturally to you. That doesn't mean you don't ever have to work at it or improve it, but it's something *you were born to do.* And even if you're not getting paid for it at the moment or you're not sure about the how's or when's of it all, keep coming back to it.

*And if you keep coming back to it* and blessing people with that particular gift and that energy, I believe that life, God, the universe (whatever you believe in) blesses you in return.
You were wired to love the things you love for a reason, even if it seems irrational or doesn't make sense right now.

There is a path unfolding. And if you keep putting that energy out into the world, I believe it always comes back to you in some form or another. Even if it's in ways you don't understand yet… In fact, it rarely turns out how you expected it to turn out. Don't let your need to control and your brain's attempts at predicting the future rob you of the magic of it all. You're fully allowed to lean into the desires of your heart, in fact, it's encouraged that you do so. If you give, the universe always makes you whole. *If you give, you will be replenished tenfold.*

Our lives are made up of *choices*. Every day, in every moment and every interaction, we *choose* to behave in a way that either reaffirms and strengthens our foundation as a powerful woman or it weakens it to the point where it crumbles. No judgment, I've disrespected myself plenty of times. Violated my boundaries and didn't speak up for myself because I was not *"in a position of power."* Said yes, when everything in me was screaming no. That's okay because when our foundations crumble, we get to build anew. You get to build a new foundation. Establish a new relationship with yourself and position yourself accordingly in the world. Your strength and your success do not depend on someone else's tolerance of your self empowered behaviour. Every single day, in every single moment, we get to choose who we want to be. Over and over again.

*Sovereignty*

True sovereignty is a state of being, not a byproduct of circumstance.
I do not become sovereign when everything in my life is perfect.
I command sovereignty even when the external world decides that I am not worthy.
I command sovereignty,
*autonomy.*
I am the queen and the commander of my emotional landscape.

If you want big, give yourself permission to want big. To live *big*. To dream *big*. If big is your heart's desire then be audacious enough to let that in fully. To trust yourself fully and throw every well-meaning limitation out the door. If you want big, then honey, I want your life to be illogical. To defy all expectations of what you get to have and how your life gets to look. If you want big wealth? Cool, claim it. If you want big love? Say it out loud. You breathe differently when you know your success is inevitable. You can *exhale*. You can *trust*. If you're doing your part and talking to God and the universe, you can breathe into knowing that you are always on your way. Give yourself permission for the big desires of your heart over and over again. Every single day. *Things get to work out in your favour if you'll let them.*

Where you're going there is no room for doubt, you're going to have to check her at the door.

Love,

B.

*Comparison* is another way of saying you don't trust where you're going. You don't trust what you're doing. You don't trust that your gifts and the energy you bring to every situation are enough. Because if this person is doing the thing I really desire then there is not enough for me. It means that all that I am when I am doing the things I am supposed to be doing and living in my purpose, *somehow won't be enough.* It's not breathtakingly unique enough. It's not enough to claim its own space. It's not enough to validate the decisions I've been making and the risks I've been taking. I'm telling you, stepping into your power looks like knowing that your place and your seat at the table are and *always have been reserved.* No need to compete with anyone for provision. The provision was already set aside for you and your heart's desire was supposed to lead you there. I trust that God always had my blessings set aside for me.

Does rejection really paralyze you? If something or someone doesn't want you, does it make you question your worth? Or worse, does it make you question your *judgment?* Make you think things like: how could I have been so foolish? Did I read all the signs wrong? I thought this thing or this person was *for me.* Here's what I learned from applying and interviewing for jobs during my last years of school: sometimes we think that if we cast our pool really *wide* and we try to appeal to a lot of people we have a better chance of finding the person or job that is right for us. If we try to be all of these "right" things and shoot our shot as much as we can then we will somehow trick the universe's timing and get what we want faster. The law of numbers. Logically, it makes sense.

*Except when we keep running into mismatches, we start to get desperate.* Why is it that all these people don't want me? And it starts to really mess with your self-worth and your self-esteem. I've learned that what is *set aside for you* will come, and it will come exactly when it's supposed to. Yes, you're supposed to do the aligned actions. But if you are trying to force a connection, you will just end up tiring yourself out, wasting a lot of energy and somehow taking on the belief that there is something wrong with you and this is just how it is for people like you.

I'm telling you that when I started to get *choosy*. And only applied to places that lit me up and felt aligned, I got the job I was meant for in every single way and it became so clear why it never would have worked with any of the others. And that applies to dating too. When I started setting my standard instead of begging for scraps and forcing them to make it work, what was meant to me came into my life. I also learned the harsh consequences that come from accepting the wrong opportunities, the ones that were not meant for me. But that's a story for another time. All I'm saying is that rejection has literally always been a blessing in my life. I just made the waiting period mean something that it never was.

There are two kinds of toxic comparison:
Comparing where you are with where you *perceive someone else is*. Comparing where you are with where you *think you should be*. Free yourself from the illusion by leaning into trust.
*You were planted in this season for a reason.*

The comparison isn't even real. We take one aspect of someone's life and compare it to the part where we think we are behind them, without taking into account that there may be other parts of their life where they could be behind you in their progress. But you don't see that because you're drawing a comparison to someone's highlight reel. You're cherry-picking your comparison. The comparison isn't even based on a full representation of that person's journey - it's just one aspect of their life that we've picked out to punish ourselves for not being what we perceive as "far enough". It's an illusion created by you. Break free by leaning into trust. You're on your own beautiful journey and on your own special timing. Invest in that. Be focused on your evolution. God planted you in your season for a reason. Trust in your journey's divine timing. Everyone else's journey is none of our business.

If you don't believe in your vision, no amount of support or encouragement from others will get you to move and make it come true.

If you fully believe in your vision, there is no amount of discouragement or lack being projected on you by others that will prevail over your life and mission.

You are certain, you are immovable.

*Unshakeable*. Rooted.

It's that simple.

Only you can believe God's calling over your life.

Your only job is to open the channel and *keep yourself open* for miracles and support.

Prioritize whatever you need to heal. Don't solicit other opinions on whether they approve of your healing.

Healing often requires changing patterns and ways of life that used to benefit the people around you.

This change may not be welcome.

Not greeted with open arms.

Heal anyway, go forth anyway.

The collective depends on it.

*I am meticulous in my craft and the experience I curate for those who choose to experience my work.* Meticulous, not a standard of perfection. *Meticulous* - Intentional. Precise. Deliberate. Everything is done with a particular energy. Delicious. Profound. When we care about something, we can get caught up in working hard for the sake of working hard. The pressure to be perfect. *Flawless.* We confuse having an impact and caring about what we do and putting our heart and soul into *what we do* with having it all figured out and doing things perfectly. Yes, do things with every detail in place for a purpose, for higher service, for a particular experience... Do your work with pride and meticulous service, but let's let go of perfection. Especially when it comes to creativity. Because all it does is drain you. It stifles and strangles the magic of the co-creative process. Let's ditch the standard of perfection for us and others and make space for grace. For magic. For the ability to be human. For the universe to be able to step in.

You are the *iconic woman.*

You may struggle, but baby you turn that pain into gold. Into purpose. Into branding.
The way you take broken shards and piece yourself back together again. A more self-possessed and fierce creature every time. The way you rise from the ashes. Your tenacity never waivers. The way you carry yourself is an art form. The way you take care of yourself. The way you *take care of people* and win their hearts over. You don't need to blow smoke up anyone's ass, your charm is magnetic. The way you embody integrity over and over, even if the world tests your patience. Your attention is exclusive. *Your focus is unmatched.* There's no obstacle you cannot conquer because you know you've already won. You have God's favor over your life.

*What desire is beneath your metric obsession?* What desire is beneath your need to get straight As? What desire is beneath your need to make x amount of dollars? To achieve x goal in your business? To get married and have 3 kids by 30? To dominate x industry? To have x amount of followers? Can you look at what need or desire is driving that whole thing? Is there a way you can fulfill that desire or need with ease? Is it something you can give yourself internally? Is it a desire or need for safety? Love? Freedom? Impact? Can you embody it? *The less you outsource your power, the closer your desire will be.* If you focus on fulfilling it within yourself, building the life you want will feel less heavy. You can do it without feeling like you're going to crumble under the pressure. It's always been for you. Focus on the desire, not the way you assume it needs to happen.

I think one of the things that trip people up in life is thinking that they are especially excluded from the magic of the universe. Like blessings and good fortune are allowed to rain down on other people, but not them. They are excluded from the miracles club. The universe could literally be shoving examples of what is possible for them right in their face - *if they would just follow their heart -* and they would say "that's because she has xyz or is xyz's son/daughter." Always coming up with reasons for which *they are different from that success story.* That love story. That story of happiness and joy. They can witness it happen for anyone or everyone around them, but they have decided that it's never allowed to happen to them. Repeating the cycle of making what is meant for them unattainable in their eyes and their minds. My darling, you are not excluded from the magic of the universe. *You are the universe.*

Your heart is your guide in this life. It connects you to all that is pure in this world - love. It makes fear a little quieter when it's in the driver's seat. Your heart will take you to the places you were meant to love living, the things you were meant to love doing, and the people you were always meant to cherish. I hope you are always heart-led in your endeavours. If you trust it, it won't steer you wrong. I've noticed that if the heart comes up against logic, a lot of people will try to quiet the inconvenient and juicy desires of the heart under the guise of logic's wisdom. I would bet on the heart every time. You see the heart is strong - it has the endurance to come up against this world's disappointments and hurts. It gets stronger with the more love it gives and receives. When you rely on logic to endure the world's landscape, you will usually find that there is not enough strength in its foundation to get you through the winters of your life. To be the source of your life.

It takes courage to pursue the life that's meant for you. You have to be willing to be wrong, *to see things differently.* You have to be willing to accept that some things are out of your control, which can be mentally terrifying when you start taking risks. You think there's a lot on the line, there's a lot to lose. You can't quite see yet that it's always adding up to your good. It takes courage to hold your own, even when it looks to the naked eye like everything is falling apart. It takes courage to have more faith, *to have trust falls with God and the universe.* Sometimes, you may even question yourself, but the extraordinary life requires more faith in what could happen than what is happening. Because if you have more faith in what you see is possible in the tangible world, you cannot create what's missing in this world. You cannot create *light* if you have more faith in the darkness. You cannot create the telephone, the internet, or medicine. You cannot create the car if you believe the only way to travel is horses. Maybe you're not inventing anything, but building an extraordinary life often looks the same. Taking step by step, moment by moment, until you get *momentum.* Sometimes, you may even have to start over. Make no mistake - every single one of those steps took massive and radical courage.

## *CLAIM IT*

Claim that you're a badass businesswoman. A compelling writer. An influencer. A painter. A singer. An artist. A visionary. I'm not talking about deciding you are something and waiting for it to happen. I'm not talking about thinking shiny thoughts. I'm talking about no longer putting down your accomplishments in front of other people. I'm talking about the things you are *already doing* but you're not as far in it yet. You haven't reached the arbitrary metric or milestone you've set as *"required"* in your head to claim it. Claim what you are doing. Claim what you have been hiding from people. You are *already doing the thing, so why not just claim the identity?* Hmm? Is it because you're afraid that if you don't check that box in your head and you've claimed it, everyone is going to see you as a failure? I am bored of talented and revolutionary people lurking in the shadows of their accomplishments because "not good enough" or imposter syndrome has claimed them. Take your power back, claim what you're already doing. You decide what identity you want to claim. *Go all in.*

*The woman for the job*

There came a point
where I had to choose to stop poisoning my mind
by believing more in limitations than I did my calling.
By believing more for the burdens and responsibilities placed upon me.
*How heavy they seemed.*
Instead, I started becoming more grateful
that I was the woman God *trusted with the job.*
With the calling.
With the work.
And I started trusting more, believing for more.
I trusted that He had provision and peace for me.
That the job wasn't mine to do alone,
*I was always divinely supported.*

You are the woman for the job, and it was uniquely tailored for your skillset, experience, and heart. You cannot fail.

Sometimes when it looks like it's all falling apart or when you think it's "not working", that is where you have to lean in more.
That is when the universe is asking you to trust more.
When you are most tempted to walk away and give up, sometimes that is the moment right before.
*Right before.*
That is the moment right before it happens.
Right before everything changes.

Holding duality - you can have things go wrong and still feel happy. Your feelings, your mind, and your state of being don't always have to follow what you see in the outside world. Sometimes you know more within yourself.

Sometimes there's a voice whispering *you've already made it out of this, don't be scared.* Sometimes there's a voice whispering *it's not as bad as it looks.*

Sometimes there's a voice whispering *it's all adding up to your favor. You can't miss the mark.* Trust that voice. Trust your voice.

*Building in suspense*

God, I am running. I am running as far away as I can from the mundane. From the things I have settled for. From the places that ask me to shrink myself. From the places that are okay, but not quite right. I am running towards what you've called me to. I don't know how it's going to work. I don't know how it's going to look. All I know is that I have a gift. I feel a stirring in my heart. I hear a voice and it's giving me a *direction*. It's giving me a direction, not a destination. So I am running in that direction and it's leading me away from all I've ever known. And it's asking me to check some mindsets at the door. And it's asking so much of me it feels like. It's asking me for strength, it's asking me for courage, it's asking me for endurance, it's asking me for *trust*. It's asking me for audacity. So I'm giving it all I've got. I'm changing my ways. And I am praying that it's all enough. And that the timing will work out in the million ways that it's supposed to. Do you feel the suspense building up? Do you feel like the clock is ticking? I'm running this - but it's not a race. And some days I need to catch my breath. I'm running this and I don't know where I am going to go or when I'm going to get there, but I know in my soul, *I'm running in the right direction.*

*Casting Worry Aside*

The bigger the calling on your life, the greater your mental stamina needs to be. A supportive mindset and mental state need to be integrated. With that I say, the knowledge that *you are not your thoughts* is part of this mental state. Knowing that certain emotions will come up, but they will not dictate our actions is part of that. A lot of times, a great calling will test you emotionally. Test your ability to trust, to cast worry and fear to the side, and your ability to continue to execute in the face of perceived adversity. The bigger the calling, the greater the pressure. The bigger the calling, the bigger the doubt and the fear. The mental traps and narratives. Bigger responsibility. All I know is that you can handle it or the calling wouldn't be on your life. Let that one simple and radical thought weave you through all the other mental illusions that present themselves on your path.

We have been sold this lie that people deciding their worth, *their intrinsic value,* is revolutionary, irrational, and dangerous. Instead, we should conform to the value a job, a market, a partner, a parent, a school or a teacher dictates. Some metrics decide our worth for us. *Your time and your labour are worth minimum wage, 45K, 100K.* We should *"take what we can get"* and consider ourselves lucky. I think not. I think God decided my worth before you ever laid eyes on me. You are worth what you decide and you will choose it every day until the world conforms.

*I hope you rise.*

I hope you rise through whatever doubts you're facing.
I hope you rise through the generational patterns that keep you down.
I hope you rise through the lack that has kept you down.
I hope you rise to the occasion.
I hope you rise to the calling on your life.
I hope you rise through the loss and the heartache.
I hope you rise in your faith.
I hope you rise to love.
I hope you rise through fear and brokenness.

*I hope you rise to whatever you're facing and heal.*

The easiest thing in the world would be to give up. To decide you're not qualified. You're not called. Return this to sender, it must have been a mistake. Wrong address, wrong person. These dreams, these demands on my life are too damn big. Don't you know what I'm facing in this world? Don't you know the competition I have? But instead of giving up, I invite you to meet life in this moment. In these delicious and beautiful and divine moments. Where everything can be still and imperfect. And instead of looking at all the ways that you cannot do the things you want to do with all your heart, I wonder if you could just take one step in this one moment. And allow yourself to be guided.

Focus on creating a message that reflects who you truly are and an audience that resonates with that message will come. Focus on creating a business that embodies your authentic energetic signature and the clients who resonate with that will come. Focus on creating a life that is authentic to what you crave in your soul and the community will find you.

The point is that your own authentic energetic signature is not only enough and *wildly* worthy, it's essential to having the things you want. Your job is to wade through the noise and bring forth what was always within you. Stop projecting what you think people want to hear or see, start projecting you.

I started leaning into being the influential woman I was born to be. *Called to be.* Started seeing myself mentally as what I was *already being.* Getting rid of the so-called humble programming in my mind that told me as a woman I could not take up space. That I shouldn't let thoughts of influence and impact get in my mind, it wasn't very classy or lady-like. Programming that tells you owning your power is filled with ego. *Couldn't be further from the truth.* I should stay in my usual lane and keep my head down while doing the work. *What I learned was that when I operate from my power is actually where I lose my ego.* It's when I forget my inherent power that I start operating from ego and trying to prove something. *Operating in lack.* I was leading myself with integrity and grace. People started looking to me as a source of something great. No ego in it, *providing value.* Holding space for others. Walking out what I've been tasked to walk out. Holding out my hand to others, *this way.* Being okay owning the energy of *influence.* Because it's not even about me anymore.

*Having a secure relationship with your greatness*

Something very interesting happens when you stop strangling the magic of the universe with demands like "when is it going to happen for me?" "How is it going to happen?" "why hasn't it happened yet" and my personal favourite: "what can I do to make it go faster?" Do I exhaust myself by working harder? Making myself unhappy and frustrated? Something very interesting happens when you live and anchor yourself in the belief that you were called for a purpose. *You don't even have to remember what it is.*

You have a choice: you can live your life from a state of impatience, control and fear. Or you could delight that you're always *on the brink of discovering another piece.* You're on the *brink of discovering the ways that the universe could delight you.* When you start having a secure relationship with your greatness, you stop strangling the magic. You don't need to be insecure - you don't need to check-in to see if you're still destined for greatness every day. Whether you're still called. You can be secure in the belief that greatness oozes from within you and it's going to happen whether you take this path or that path. When you stop trying to control everything, *something very interesting happens*: you get where you need to go. The place you were always going to end up. You just get there faster and with more joy.

Something is intoxicating about your company.

Your energy.

What a gift to be in your presence.

Save it for those who will cherish this.

*Playing in leading energy.*

I feel like the call to lead has been inundated with heavy and unattainable energy. So people don't want to claim it even if they are already leading. It couldn't be as simple as kindness and integrity. It couldn't be as simple as modelling behaviour and standards for life that are positive and worth aspiring to. It couldn't be as simple as radical compassion for your fellow humans and outstretching our hands to help those we can help. It couldn't be as simple as having grace and forgiving. Following what lights us up in this world and letting other people bask in that light. *Sharing.* Opening space in communities. Showing people that they can also claim joy in their own lives. That it's there in all seasons. And the torch that's passed down doesn't have to be carried alone. The call to lead doesn't have to swallow your whole identity. Maybe the call to lead is *part* of your identity. Figure out how you can make it more you. Being more you is how you lead. Sharing your truth. Sharing all that you are. *Maybe that is leadership.*

Letting yourself be seen requires a lot of self-trust, but you can handle it. We shrink away from being seen because being seen can mean we're on display. People can see us. This means they can also judge us, label us, project onto us, and *gasp* dislike us. Most of us are wired to want to be liked. But here's the thing - you owe yourself the freedom of being seen. The freedom that comes with being yourself fully and being authentic to who you are. When you are called to lead, people will judge you no matter what call you make. *It comes with the territory.* Even if you do nothing, people may judge, label or dislike you. You can handle it. You trust yourself. And the life that is waiting for you is worth having a few critics. In fact, you're probably doing something right if there are a few people out there who are getting triggered by your success. Bask in your own glow. It's none of your business what anyone else thinks.

*I can handle it*

Adversity will quiver in your presence.

When you start saying "I can handle it - no matter what happens I know I can handle it. I am deeply supported by God and the universe," rather than saying *"what if"* and feeding the energy of "everything in this life is more powerful than me". *My circumstances are more powerful than me.* Feeding the energy of "what if it doesn't work out," "it probably won't work out" "look, this didn't work out so it's more evidence that it won't work out." Start feeding the energy of no matter what the outcome, I can handle it. I can handle myself. I can trust myself. I've faced the darkness before, but now I'm choosing to trust the light.

*Highest standards for the Highest woman*

Highest standards for the Highest woman. The highest version of yourself. The highest standards to create an inner environment she can thrive in. So she can settle in. You know how you are when your standards and boundaries are weak. When you allow yourself to be swept up by life. We can go through difficult seasons, have difficult moments, and difficult years, but we can't stay there. Whether you are writing a bestseller, becoming a coach, running for office, or starring in a box office hit, it's going to require that you raise your standards for yourself. That you seek expansion and lead with integrity. That you draw her out; that version of you that's required for this next part.

Sorry babe, you are the self-led woman.

So it won't satisfy you to follow someone else's path.

The conventional path. You blaze your own trails.

Your heart and your soul will lead you down some unfamiliar terrain.

In this game of life, *you're going off-roading to win.*

You need to own your desires before you can possess them.
You go nowhere by pretending you don't want what you want.
Your desires are waiting for you to own them.
To hold them in your hand.

*Liberation*

There is a quiet revolution in *undressing*.
Shedding all that you have been asked to be.
All that weighs on your Spirit.
*Unbecoming.*

Presenting yourself to the world with a naked authenticity.
Clothed only in self-acceptance.
Disrobing,
stripping away every identity that was never even yours.
Freedom exists in allowing yourself to be seen.

Care for yourself enough not to let people's reactions to who you, or *their perception of whom they think you are,* make you crumble. *Compromise your identity.* Make you want to get small and hide. Run in the opposite direction of your dreams. *Chase you out of your own spaces.* Adopt a new voice, a new tone. A smaller posture. Deceive you into thinking you're not good enough. Your life, your impact, and your calling are so much bigger than you know.

Empowerment is a posture. A way of being. A way of moving through the world. An energy. So are lack, insecurity, and unworthiness. They're a slouch. And they bring an energy of stagnation to your life, *where nothing can grow.* The same way that you can change the way you're sitting at any moment, you can correct your energy. Correct your posture. Sometimes, all it takes is to raise your chin to look straight ahead at the world. Sometimes, it requires figuring out where your body is contracting and straightening your spine. Other times, it requires removing from your life whatever keeps your eyes and attention fixed on the ground, rather than what's right in front of you.

Nothing will stop you from moving forward quite like retracing your steps. Replaying mistakes. Assuming that all you'll ever get in this life is what you've always received. The past is your barrier to the future. You will never arrive at your desired future, or even live in the present for that matter, if you keep recreating the past. Trying to fix it, trying to do it differently. Different people, same scenarios. Different jobs, same scenarios. Different city, same scenarios. Sometimes the scenarios may even look different, but it's the same triggers playing out. You're going to need to *consciously* reassess and address what you're *expecting* from life. From yourself. From other people. What you're projecting, the patterns that have become entrenched in your mind. The only way forward is to drop the past. *Not fight it, not analyze it to death.* Let it go. Accept that it no longer gets to dictate what your future looks like.

*Letters to myself*

*Do you love her?* The woman staring back at you in the mirror? Those deep brown *(tired)* eyes and that beautiful warm smile? You do?

Okay, then give her some more grace. Don't be so hard on her. Give her more room to breathe when she's made a mistake. She's learning, you know. You're so easy to forgive other people, but you're so slow to forgive yourself. She's trying to do better every day. She's worthy of your fierce compassion.

Cut her some slack.

She's a woman, not a machine.

She's working tirelessly to make your dreams a reality. She's breaking generational curses.

She's learning how to be of this world, but not so attached to everything in it.

She's had her heart broken and her fair share of disappointments.

*You expect a lot from her.*

But you also need to give her some grace. Some peace. Some rest.

Because you can't get anywhere if you exhaust her.

Because you can't get anywhere without her.

If you love her, you'll give her peace.

Stop making the timing of your life mean something. It doesn't mean anything. We would save ourselves a lot of unnecessary suffering if we stopped deciding that if something doesn't happen by our imaginary timeline, *it's never going to happen*. So we should just throw in the towel. This is what makes you give up and walk away from things just as they are about to transpire. The universe is just looking at you confused like "I thought you wanted this? You said you wanted this?" then shrugs and walks away. Like, we throw a tantrum because if it didn't happen by Tuesday, November 31st at 6 pm, then that automatically means we're a failure and our dreams are dead. I'm trying to be funny here, but seriously, if some of the greats decided to give up on their life's work because things weren't working on their timeline, humanity would be robbed of many valuable things and no one would ever know of those people. Think about that. You're allowed to rest and reassess, but don't give up. Don't let it mean you're unworthy, unqualified, and over.

*Divine Intelligence*

Loosen your grip. *Relax.* Return within your body. Reoccupy yourself. Make space within your mind for something else to come through. The part of you that's not connected to the world you're experiencing, but something greater. The part of you that is the universe. Make way within yourself. Roll out the red carpet, my love. Make way for divine intelligence. A partnership worthy of your embrace. It's all connected to your calling, to your purpose, to your return. Make way for the creative energy you're housing. Make way for your divine insights, your intuition, *all that brings you back home to yourself.* Make way. Make room, *it needs space to breathe.* It needs space to come through you. Make way. Clear the clutter that comes from worry, fear, and shame. Clear your mind of your conditioning *even just for a moment.* Clear your mind from the logical and make space for your divine intelligence. Welcome to your creative matrix.

There are things in your life that will be borne of the need to survive. You know, the mental patterns, the safety mechanisms, the places you have to lock yourself up mentally for your ego to keep you safe from yourself. *From the hurt you've been through.* There are things in your life that started to grow because all you knew was instability, chaos and lack. Those basic needs of yours were not met. But the next part of your life gets to be something different - the next part of your life, you get to choose supportive inner environments. You get to create things in your life from a place of magic, trust, and joy. From an energy of peace, tranquility, and luxury. You get to open your heart to the desires that you banished long ago because it didn't seem safe to even *think about them,* let alone utter them out loud. You get to make different choices now. *The next part of your life can be born of love, rather than fear.*

What is inspiration, other than a blessing from the divine? A touch from the divine?

A kiss from your muse?

How lucky you are to have been chosen to bring this into the world.

This particular idea. This particular book. This particular song. This particular painting.

A stroke of genius. A stroke of luck.

How beautiful it is to have known such favor.

The universe's gift to my heart.

To know purpose, to know creation, to know art.

You, my love, have a gift just waiting to be shared with the world.

Don't keep it locked up.

Let it be known, on display for its beautiful majesty,

the onlookers are changed

from what you have borne and birthed into reality.

*A philosopher's conundrum*

I think that for me, going after my dream life was initially motivated by the desire *for freedom*. A refusal to feel confined to any type of life or to anyone's whim. I'll call it a repulsion to dependency. Because I saw what it looks like to depend on things. To have the rules of the game change before your very eyes because you're not the one who's in control. Jumping through someone else's hoops. To be dependent on material circumstances, to jobs, and still to never have enough. *Lack, lack, lack, lack.* I saw what it looked like to *work hard*, to cooperate, to play the rules of the game, but never have enough. *Work, work, work, work.* To sacrifice everything. To be forced into playing the game that our society has set up for us. So when I grew up, my motivator was to do everything in my power to stop living in a cage. Both physically and mentally. To *leave the cave*. A philosopher's conundrum.

*The Enlightened Woman*

Ah, the enlightened woman. The enlightened woman, the Queen.
She is not one who has never been touched by fear.
Neither, one who has left fear's grasp.
No, she is one who has embraced fear.
She welcomes fear into her kingdom.
Sits with fear,
but does not let fear give orders or run the kingdom.
The Queen has trained fear like a dog, so that fear knows its place.
The Queen has made fear her bitch.

*The Entitled Woman*

She is here to collect on her entitlements. Enforce her birthrights.
She will not be cheated or scammed out of her purpose.
Collect on the debts her ancestors have already paid for.
She has come for her promise of abundance, the life she was always destined to live.
"No" is not an acceptable part of her vocabulary.
You're already been outwitted and outmatched with this one.
She always gets what she came for.
Watch how you treat her, she's a formidable enemy if you make her one.

*Divinely Supported*

The impact you're going to make.
The story you're going to tell.
The legacy you're going to leave behind.
The courage you're going to possess.
The people you're going to inspire.
The vision you're going to follow.
The purpose you're going to live out.
It seems so scary. So much bigger than you.
Because you were never meant to do it on your own.
You are more divinely supported than you could
*ever imagine.*

My heart goes out to the ones who are tasked with doing something different. The ones who have big dreams and vision, but no support around them. They've never seen it done before. It takes so much strength and courage to be the first in your family or community to do something. To go after a dream. To break a pattern. Everything you want seems so big that it's easier to ignore the vision than to take the unknown path alone. But I'm here to tell you that you are not alone. And the path is already unfolding.

*Ode to the "Self-Made" Woman*

Here's the thing about us self-made women: we have gone without. So when we get everything we desire in this life, we still have memories of what it's like to have nothing.

We have memories of what it was like when we were still building and dreaming up our lives.
We went through things that ripped us apart in ways that we couldn't even utter. We sacrificed things.

All so we can have the capacity to appreciate the gifts we would be blessed with.
*So that the light could fill us up in all dark places.*

So we could become the woman who gets everything she wants,
but understands what it means to go without
and vividly remembers what it's like to be on her knees,
crying out.
For us, abundance may have come at a price.

Self-made women, we are haunted by the memories of where we came from
and what we had to let go of *to get here.*

Release the expectation that it has to happen a certain way. *That what you desire in life can only come from following one path.* One path to success. One path to happiness. One path to fulfillment. One path to your dream job. One path to your dream relationship. Release the unhelpful assumption that you must know and control every detail in your life for your desires to come to you. You're putting all the pressure and all the work on yourself. This is a safety mechanism your brain has picked up, but it doesn't have to be true. You can be safe in the world. You can create safety within yourself. And from there, your life can open up. *You can do the divine work from a state of peace and ease.* Let the magic of life blow you away when you allow the universe to take the reins.

Many of us observed and adopted the energetic standards of our parents and the people closest to us. We observed their standard for money, friendships, and relationships as children. As adults, we unconsciously mimic this standard in our lives. And then when we want more for our lives, we feel shame. What makes us special enough or more worthy? To want more than our parents got in this life? Do we think we are more worthy than the people who gave us life? Then this becomes our trap and our ceiling. We meet the edge then we decide not to go further. Be aware of the way this may manifest in your life. Are you setting your own energetic standard or are you taking on the standards of someone you admire/love/care for that is close to you? It's not about comparing yourself to anyone else. Your heart's desires are worthy because they are. Everyone's desires are their own unique blueprint. Comparison and shame were something we inserted later.

Use faith as your life raft if you are wading through deep waters of doubt and fear.

If you keep moving towards the light, you'll eventually find yourself in more

*shallow waters.*

Even if you feel lost, faith ensures you will be *found.*

God put drive in me. So I would lay awake at night and ask myself the hard questions. So that I'd make sure I was grateful but never complacent. So I would lay awake at night and wonder if I was living my purpose. My calling. If I was doing what He wanted me to. Whether I was living the way He had designed me; using the gifts and capabilities that He gave me in order to make the world better. Was I doing enough? And the truth was that I was doing too much and too little *in the right direction*. Us, the women with the obsessive drive and passion to serve and do it all, we need to make more space in our lives to receive. We need to make more space for ease. We need to make more space for peace. Go to sleep, rest your eyes and your mind.

I hope you choose to live boldly. Live a *fucking* bold life. I hope you chase your passions and your loves with a full and open heart. I hope you walk out the steps your heart designed with your blessed intuition guiding you, *holding your hand through it all.* I hope that when the world tells you no, you know it's always going to be a *not yet,* but almost. Until one day it's a y e s. I hope you learn that trusting yourself is your only damn job every day, all day. Even if you've made mistakes before, you can choose to start fresh at any given moment. I hope you do make mistakes. Because you're human. You'll learn from it and you can handle it. *Mistakes are a sign that you had the courage to try something.*

This is for the ones who just couldn't leave well enough alone. The ones that had a longing. A frustration. A desire that just kept pulling at them and left them unsatisfied. Kept them up at night. Had their blood boiling. Sometimes, I think it's like playing a game of hot and cold. The closer your desire, the more heated you get. The more frustrated you can get. *It's leading you. You're getting warmer and warmer.* Don't quit now. It's a full-body feeling, sometimes you could mistake it for a fever dream. Burning up for what was placed on your soul, in your body, and in your heart. It's got its hold on you. It always has. You're so close. Almost there. *You're in the moment right before it happens.* Right before it materializes. Its energetic essence matched to you and you to it. Tasked with finding each other, you sense it when it's near. Sometimes, your dissatisfaction is leading you. You've been equipped with it so that you don't stop until you find your target. *Until you find what you were made for.*

When you're *living and breathing* in your zone of genius, the universe gives you deposits. Some might call it alignment, others will call it inspiration. Call it whatever you want, but that's how you know. When you're just *living* - eating, sleeping, or driving your car - and it's just an overflow of downloads. You *live* in the place of overflow. Your job is to withdraw and share. Your gifts are how the divine chooses to communicate with you. You are chosen for your journey. Your gifts, a means of communication. A means of shifting in and out of frequencies. You are so loved by the Most High. This is how you unlock your codes in yourself and for others.

Finding yourself doesn't happen all at once.

Neither does self-abandonment.

We *vacate ourselves in small acts of betrayal*

bit by bit

until all we carry is an empty vessel

we no longer recognize.

The good news is that coming back to yourself

works just the same.

In small steps and choices,

every day.

Until you're *whole again.*

Until you're at home within yourself *once again.*

The dark will teach you to celebrate the light.

*You will develop gratitude.*
Being lost will teach you to seek your path.
*You will develop direction.*
The noise in your mind will teach you to hone in on one voice with your whole being.
*You will develop focus.*

What you're going through is not for nothing.
You're collecting experience,
*you're collecting ingredients.*

People assume that living out your calling is going to take a lot from you. It's going to take a lot of energy. It's going to take a lot of work. You know what else takes a lot of energy? *Regret.* Repressing what is a part of you. Repressing who you are. Living a life that never feels quite right. Mediocre discontent. It's a deep discomfort that you walk around with. Believe me, although your calling may require you to break and expand over and over, this will come more naturally to you than complete self-abandonment.

*For the woman who sets herself on fire for what she loves*

The flames do not have to consume you.
Learn to
*harness that energy*
to build something
timeless,
*everlasting.*
That which will exist beyond time and space.
The impact stretches forward beyond
your lifetime.
*Cascading into the future.*

*Medicine for when it hurts*

When your heart is broken,
when things don't go your way,
wrap yourself in a blanket of compassion and
*understanding.*
Hold yourself while you cry.
Be *your own space* for healing and emotional outpour.
Sing to yourself.
Fill your brain with words of love and affirmation.

And *when it's time, trade your pain for peace*
because you cannot hold onto both.

Fill yourself to the brim with love and compassion.

*The Courage to Live*

I don't think courage always means slaying dragons or going to battle.
Courage means daring to say what's in your heart.
*Making yourself vulnerable.*
Standing up for what you believe in, even when other people *disagree.*

It means being the fullest and truest expression of who you really are and fighting for the life you know you are capable of living. Despite what those closest to you have said about your *worth.*

It means loving again even after you've been broken
and you've cried so hard you had to gasp for air.
Fighting internal demons; crippling anxiety and fear.
Creating or building something new that you've never seen done before even when you're scared and unsure of what it will turn into. Taking up space when you've been taught to be small.

I think living, *truly living,* takes immense courage these days. Whether you know it or not, *you are so brave.*

Have you ever loved something (or maybe someone) in such a grand and illogical way? Like, have you ever had a passion that was just constantly calling to you? I mean, you could put it in a box and walk away, but it's just *always speaking to you.* Whenever you abandon it (*because it's rarely practical*), you feel the pull. It makes my skin crawl. My blood boil. It feels like my whole being is calling me to it. *Maybe for you, it's more peaceful, like a humming that's within you.* But it's not something I can find in the outside world. Me and my passion, we are one and the same. It's one entity. It's something that I cannot be at peace within myself if it's not a part of my life. Because without it, I am not fully myself. I feel like, if you know what I'm talking about, it's because we're wired a certain way. Like for the rest of our lives, our purpose is to make space for the thing we love within our lives in *some way* and have it lead us wherever God has planned for us. But I know, for the rest of my life I'm married to this passion of mine. This is a commitment I made before this lifetime. A safe guidance system. If there is something within you that speaks to you in this way, follow it until it gets louder. And when it gets louder, let it in. Because it won't find you until you go looking for it. *This one's an internal journey.* My passion is a partnership with the divine, so it makes space for the illogical.

*In defense of the in-between,*

Everyone hates the in-between phase. We like the start, like the start of a relationship, we are wide-eyed and excited. Endorphins pumping. In the beginning, we are full of zest and ready to do the work. Then the middle comes and we feel like it's a damn slog. A grind. The middle feels so far from where we wanted to go. How fast we thought we would get there. The destination feels out of reach. *Oh, what's that?* Feeling discouraged. Impatient. Growing pains are uncomfortable. We just want to get to the end of the ride. The in-between takes a commitment that not a lot of people want to put in. But the in-between is actually where you cultivate what is required and necessary to be able to handle the destination.

*I'll do whatever it takes / Power Moves*

"I'll do whatever it takes to realize my heart's desires" is an energy. It's a command that the universe responds to. It's bold. It's daring. It takes courage. It's audacious. It unlocks doors. Because it says, universe I am ready for your guidance. I am also ready to do my part. Do the action, and put things in motion, *even if it feels illogical and impractical.* I'm willing to throw my limitations out the door and adopt a mind that is limitless and abundant. *In a world that is constantly feeding me limitation and lack, this is a power move.* Because I know what I am meant to have and I am willing to receive it. I am willing to adopt a mind that doesn't make any sense to other people. Because this is what it takes to have the desires of my heart. *This is powerhouse energy.*

I burn bridges - I am focused on moving forward, not making sure I have a convenient route back to things God already showed me weren't right for me. I am focused on growing, not making sure that I will have a security blanket waiting for me if I ever feel the need to *backslide*. Your future is rarely found in rekindling the past. And even if something in your past should become your future, it has to become a whole new creation. *Nothing like it used to look* to become your future. To *service your growth*. There's a reason why it didn't work out the first time. Stop being so busy trying to check if the past will take you back and focus on building your future.

*For the Creatress*

Your role on this earth is to pursue your creativity.
Birth what was gifted to you by the divine.
*Lead with my heart.*
Bring to life hope, love, healing, and empowerment.
This is your fuel. This is where you source your power.
I honour my light and let it spill out of me.
*A sensual practice.*
Dripping in all that you are.
I protect my energy and guard my creativity against consumption that would compromise my being and taint my creative process.

*Thoughts from a Cubicle*

What if I'm standing on the precipice of greatness? But I'm too scared to ever jump in and find out? What if I'm standing at the edge of destiny, but I keep walking the line for the rest of my life instead of jumping into my calling? What if?

But, what if there's actually nothing on the other side to catch me and I've just jumped off a cliff? What if it's just deafening silence?

*I'd say it's better to jump than to feel like you're walking a tightrope your whole life.*

It can be wildly hurtful when the people closest to you put down your dreams. When they make you feel *silly* for trusting yourself. Scarcity is taught, sometimes through generations. It's hard when your *family* teaches you that there is more to fear in the world than within you to trust. You can want certain things - you just can't want *that thing.* You can't desire what is in your heart, but as an alternative, you can desire this family-stamped approved goal. *Bet on you.* Every single time. The alternative will always lead you down a path of dissatisfaction that will ultimately drive you back to your original God gifted desire. If no one has ever told you yet: *you can trust yourself.* I know you've been taught otherwise a million times, but my darling, the best thing you can do for yourself is to trust that no matter what obstacles may arise, every single time, you are worthy of your own trust. You have divine capacity.

Not being the best at something doesn't mean you're not called to make an impact. You don't have to be undefeated or the conqueror of your industry to be called to the industry. To have a place reserved for you. To be successful and happy in your own right. You don't have to be the best to be the only one who can do it like you can. You don't have to be the best to add *value*. To change *lives*. Don't miss out on your calling to temporarily shield your fragile ego. Try something. See what happens.
Don't let the fear of not being perfect paralyze you.
Get off your ass and do the work.
Respectfully,

B.

I've learned to charge head-on when it comes to the desires of my heart. And I can recognize that they are the desires of my heart because I've had *so few* that I've carried in my heart throughout the decades. I've learned to charge headfirst. Start doing things, moving stuff. Make it messy and hope things start falling into place as I go. And they always do. It rarely turns out how you thought, but if you keep executing and believing in it, it comes true. Always. I am convicted in my belief that we were gifted our desires so that we can live them out. Not so they can die, *buried,* in our hearts and minds.

Stop focusing on racking your brain to find solutions to perceived problems. Instead, focus on strengthening your connection to the divine in these moments of disempowerment. Once you plug back in, the solution to your problem will appear. You will call it intelligence or critical thinking. You are partially correct. *It's receiving your divine intelligence communicated as wisdom.*

Be a force to be reckoned with.
A force for good. For kindness.
A *conduit for healing.* For love. For empowerment.
Someone out there is waiting for you to step into your power so you can help them step into theirs. You've been gifted with talent (*I know you have)*, passion, and drive.
You've been gifted a fierce, yet kind spirit. And I believe it's your absolute responsibility to share that with the world.

## ABOUT THE GUIDED WORD

*Getting to know the visionary and the purpose behind the brand.*

**Beatrica Vasic** is the writer and creator behind *The Guided Word*, a home for creativity, empowerment and divine inspiration. It is a growing brand for bold spirit-led individuals looking to evolve, lead and step into their power. The Powerhouse woman is the self-proclaimed queen of "it shouldn't have worked, but it did."

With a passion for personal development, spirituality and writing, Bea has curated a unique online space that supports creatives and entrepreneurs on their empowerment journey as they build their brand. *The Guided Word* has amassed a sizeable audience on Instagram and has been featured in magazines.

If you liked *The Powerhouse Collection*, you can head over to Bea's corner of the internet and pull up a chair at @theguidedword on Instagram.

www.ingramcontent.com/pod-product-compliance
Lightning Source LLC
Chambersburg PA
CBHW072052110526
44590CB00018B/3131